project PHILIPPIANS

Written by **Brian Parfitt**
with additional material by
David Day and **Robin Fletcher**
Design by **Andrew Flowers**

ISBN **0 907750 583**

CPAS
Adult Training and Resources Unit
Athena Drive
Tachbrook Park
WARWICK
CV34 6NG

Tel: (0926) 334242

Reprinted 1991, 1992

Church Pastoral Aid Society
A company limited by guarantee
Registered Charity No. 1007820

CPAS

Bible Study ought to be exciting! And life changing, that is the aim of Project Philippians.

In CPAS we want to help church groups not only with their Bible Study but also with the worship, the prayer and the sharing.

For leaders a good way of learning is by doing. This course trains house group leaders in how best to lead.

There's plenty of variety here and you can select the things which will help your group grow in faith.

Paul Simmonds, Adult Training and Resources Unit. 1990.

CONTENTS

HOW TO USE THIS BOOK

It contains a series of six studies, each of which is a complete unit, but they also follow on from one another. Within each section you will find.

ON THE first two pages

aim The main point which should emerge from that week's study.

introduction Some general points about the passage as a whole and guidelines on the studies themselves.

bible notes Explanation of individual verses to give you a fuller understanding of the passage. You may like to read some of these out to the group when it would help.

sunday extra Ideas for adapting the theme for Sunday Worship either before or after the group meetings. (Suitable hymns are listed in the **worship & prayer** section).

THE next page is the...

group sheet This may be photocopied so that all the members of the group can see it. (This is an exception to the copyright. Please see details in copyright note on the title page.)
It has all the basic material for a Bible study on the week's passage and contains

begin here Discussion starters, often of a general nature, helping people to share their own experience and to begin to think about the topic.

bible study Questions which help the group to explore the meaning and message of the passage.

action Steps to take to apply what has been learned in a practical way.

ON the opposite page, for easy reference by the group leader, there are

additional questions These are more practically related or dig deeper into the text. You can integrate some of these with the questions on the worksheet or work through them separately, especially if you want a study that goes a little deeper. This could be an alternative Bible study to the one on the **group sheet**.

worship & prayer Ideas to help the group worship and pray together, including hymns and songs (all to be found in Mission Praise 1 or 2) which can be used at the meeting or during Sunday Worship.

more learning activities.
These are alternative approaches to the study of the passage, which are activity rather than discussion based.

HOW DO I PREPARE TO LEAD THE GROUP?

1 PREPARE YOURSELF

Pray about the passage, the study, the group and yourself as leader.

Work quickly through the **group sheet**, as if you were an ordinary group member. Jot down notes, questions, and areas to expand or work on. Be honest with yourself and let God teach you as you prepare.

Again read through the appropriate passage and the introductory notes.
Be guided by the **aim** and the **introduction**.

2 PLAN YOUR APPROACH

Decide how you are going to tackle the study. There are a number of possible approaches to each passage. You may decide to take two weeks over a section in order to make use of several of them.

As well as the basic Bible Study on the **group page** you might also want to select some of the **additional questions** you think may be helpful, either for using while you are discussing the **group sheet** questions or separately afterwards. Always leave the **action** section to last but leave enough time for this.

Look at the pages with **more learning activities** and see whether your group would learn more by doing the activities there. Be adventurous sometimes! Bible study need not be all 'sitting and discussing questions'. Many imaginative ways of learning have been developed for adults and these activities will help you think about Biblical principles in a deep way. Full instructions are given. Adapt the activities to suit your group but don't try and make them too easy. People like a challenge! Make sure you always do **begin here**, and **read** the passage.

3 ASSESS THE TIMING

You will not have time to cover all the material so don't set out thinking this is the aim. Marks will not be deducted if the paper is not completed! You need to use what is appropriate and helpful to your group. Think carefully about the timing of each section. We have not put down suggestions for times, since each group will have different priorities. However we suggest you WRITE DOWN, as you prepare, your target time for each section.

Try to keep to a basic framework each week and allocate times for prayer, reading, discussion, coffee, etc. even though you may feel a longer prayer time, for example, is appropriate on some occasions. It is good to end promptly so that those who need to do so can go, leaving others to chat if they wish.

ACKNOWLEDGEMENTS

We are very grateful to all those who have helped in the production of **Project Philippians**: the **Rev. Robin Fletcher** who allowed us to incorporate his Bible Study material into the studies; **David Day** who wrote the Learning Activities; **Tina Shell** and **Sarah Wylie** who have typed and retyped it all; the groups who have acted as guinea pigs at various stages of its development; **Andrew Flowers** who has done the design, and finally **Barbara Pashley**, who is the efficient secretary who gets everything organised. Even a small book like this shows the necessity of working together for which Paul calls in this letter to the Philippians!

INTRODUCING PHILIPPIANS

Faith under pressure

"A good old moan" seems to be the normal basis for conversation in Britain. We complain about the weather, about our aches and pains, the government, the trains, the buses, our children, our parents .... If we listened carefully to ourselves we would perhaps see just how negative about life we often are. If we were honest, however, we would see just how little we really have to complain about - as we often say, "There's always those worse off than yourself." Paul was someone who learned how to triumph, even in very difficult circumstances. When he wrote this letter he was in prison facing a possible death sentence. He had often encountered real difficulties - opposition and physical persecution, hunger and thirst and the pressures of life as a leader in the early church - bringing people to faith, helping them grow and worrying when things went wrong.

Paul the enthusiast

These were the things Paul faced. If he had been us he would have been in the depths of despair! Instead this letter bounces with a joy and an enthusiasm which comes from his relationship to Christ. Facing death he says, "For me to live is Christ, to die is gain." Facing opposition he says, "I count it all as loss in order to know Christ." Facing hunger he says, "I can do all things in him who strengthens me." He calls on his readers to, "Rejoice in the Lord always". As we face our problems Paul's letter encourages us to trust in Christ with the same joyful faith and to share our faith with others, as he was doing even in prison.

Paul the pastor

The letter also shows Paul's concern for the Christians in Philippi. We see his pastoral concern time and time again. He expresses the depth of his love for them; his concern for their spiritual growth. He helps them face up to the problems of opposition, of disunity, of false teaching. His concern for individuals is seen in his words about Epaphroditus and Timothy, in Chapter 2 and Euodia and Syntyche in Chapter 4. He expresses his appreciation of the financial support they had sent to him. We see the very close bond between Paul and those in his care. These passages therefore have a challenge for us about the life of our fellowships and our concern for others.

It is a very Christ-centred letter but at the same time it is very practical and challenging and will help us as we seek to live out the Christian life to the full.

1

Keep in touch!

Philippians 1.1 - 11

AIM To discover the sort of concern we should have for other Christians.

INTRODUCTION John Donne's words, "No man is an island," have become a well-worn cliche - nevertheless it is still true that we need other people. This is particularly true in our Christian lives. When we become Christians we automatically become part of the Body of Christ. Even leading Christians like Paul needed the support and help which he gained from other Christians. They were "partners" with him in his ministry through their prayer and support. He had founded the church in Philippi and brought many of them to faith, so there was a very special bond which showed itself in his concern for their growth. He wrote this letter to encourage them. Paul obviously worried about the churches and Christians he knew - but he also had confidence that in the end they were in God's hands (see verse 6).

We should have a similar concern for those Christians with whom we have links - members of our housegroup and church, those whom we have led to faith, Christian friends who live elsewhere. Like Paul we should be concerned that they go on growing as Christians and should be supporting and encouraging them in doing so. Sometimes we may lose touch, sometimes they may seem to be far away from God - in which case we need to trust that they are in God's hands and he will fulfill his purpose in their lives.

Our study this week begins with the idea of keeping in touch with friends and goes on to look at Paul's concern for the Philippian Christians and the concern we should have for our fellow Christians. Don't take too much time over the first three sections of the Bible Study on the Letter, the Writer and the Readers - they are to set the background for your study of the whole letter. Do give plenty of time to the section on "The Prayer" and to the Action section.

NOTES

v.1: The word for "servants" is in Greek the word for a slave - someone completely belonging to another person and obedient to them. It is a reflection of Paul's humility and his submission to God.

Philippi in Macedonia was founded by Philip, the father of Alexander the Great. In 42 B.C. it became a Roman colony so its citizens were treated as if they were in Italy, with all the rights of Roman citizens. Acts 16 tells the story of the foundation of the church in Philippi when Paul went over to Macedonia in response to the vision he had at Troas.

"Saints" does not imply moral holiness but that they belong to God and therefore are "holy" people.

"Bishops" means overseers. As he uses the plural the church has a group of bishops, and so he is not talking about the sort of bishops we have today. In other letters he speaks of the elders of the church - as a group they were responsible for the supervision of the life of the congregation.

"Deacons" are probably those who had a more administrative role within the community.

v.2: "Grace" was the common Greek greeting. "Peace" (Shalom) was the Jewish greeting and Paul combines the two in a characteristic way which reminds his readers of the richness of God's love for them. Grace is God's love freely given to them. Peace is the result of Christ's reconciling work.

vv.3-4: Paul begins most of his letters with thanksgiving for the Christians to whom he was writing and mention of his prayer for them. His thankfulness was not just formal but real. Prayer is one way we can help those we do not see regularly.

v.5: The Philippians showed their "fellowship" and partnership in a very practical way by the support they gave to Paul in his ministry in other places.

v.6: Paul's confidence for their future growth and progress depends not on their efforts but on God's power at work in them. The process begun at their conversion will be completed at "the day of Jesus Christ" - that is, when Jesus comes again and God's work of transforming his people is completed.

v.7: The Philippians have shared in the disgrace of Paul's imprisonment by standing by him, as partners (the word echoes the "fellowship" or "partnership" of v.5) sharing in God's grace which has helped and supported him. Though it is Paul who is on trial, he speaks of it as the Gospel being tried and vindicated.

v.8: The Christian's experience of love and compassion for others is motivated and empowered by Christ's love. Indeed his love is shown through us.

v.9: Love is the hall-mark of true discipleship but it is not an undiscriminating love. It is also seen in the decisions Christians make based on their knowledge of God and his character and their ability to distinguish right from wrong.

v.10: The word "approve" has the sense of prove in experience, not just in theory.
The word "blameless" can mean "without stumbling" or "not causing others to stumble" - an expression of love for others.

v.11: The "righteousness" Paul speaks of here is not our moral uprightness but the right standing before God made possible by Christ. That, however, should lead to changed lives, to the harvest and fruit of the Spirit described by Paul in Galatians 5.22-24. As the harvest is given by God, the praise for it should go to God.

SUNDAY EXTRA

Today's sermon could explore the theme of the Bible Study by looking at practical ways in which we can support one another as Christians or it could take a different angle on the passage and look at the description of the Christians in the passage as:

1. People who belong to God (vv.1-2)
2. People who know God's power (vv.3-8)
3. People who show God's life (vv.9-11)

For a Family Service you could use this week as a missionary focus. Talk about Paul as a missionary linked to the church in Philippi, through letters, giving and prayer (using appropriate pictures) - tie this in with the support of your church for particular missionaries or societies.

You could use audio-visual material from a society you support or focus on an individual missionary link with a report from them or an interview with someone who keeps in touch with them.

Prayer for Christian friends and the church's mission would be relevant, as well as for Christian growth (as in verses 9-11). Church Family Worship sections 12 and 25 may be suitable. Other hymns and songs listed in the Worship and Prayer section overleaf could be used.

Group Sheet 1

Keep in touch!

Philippians 1.1 - 11

AIM To discover the sort of concern we should have for our fellow Christians.

BEGIN HERE Think of the friend you have known longest. When did you last see each other? How do you keep in touch? Talk about these friends in twos and threes.

BIBLE STUDY
READ PHILIPPIANS 1.1-11

THE LETTER
Who wrote this letter?
To whom is this letter written?
Where is Philippi?
How do we keep in touch with Christian friends?

THE WRITER
If this passage was the only source for our knowledge of Paul what would we know about him?

1

2

3

4

Any more?

THE READERS
What does this passage tell us about the Christians in Philippi?

1

2

3

4

Any more?

THE PRAYER
If Paul was praying verse 9 for our church, what would we look for as evidence that his prayers were being answered?
What does it mean to be growing in
- love
- knowledge
- depth of insight?

Why are these qualities important?

ACTION On a scale of 1 - 10 (1 is weak, 10 is strong)

Is our Church growing in love?

1 ________________________________ 10

Is our church growing in knowledge?

1 ________________________________ 10

Is our church growing in depth of insight?

1 ________________________________ 10

How do we show our partnership in the Gospel today?

1

ADDITIONAL QUESTIONS

- What can we learn from verse 1 about Christian ministry?
- What was Paul's confidence about the Christians at Philippi (verse 6)? How can that confidence encourage us in our concern for our fellow-Christians?
- How does this passage illustrate our total dependence on God's grace and power?
- How do we respond to Christians in difficult circumstances? Are we ashamed of them? Do we ignore them? Do we stand with them as the Philippians did with Paul (v.7)? What are the gains of so doing?
- How do we develop the sort of discernment Paul is speaking about in verses 9- 11?
- What ways have you found helpful in praying for Christian friends and the church's mission?

WORSHIP AND PRAYER

Have a time of thanksgiving and praise for our fellowship in the body of Christ and especially for Christian friends. Take Paul's prayer in verses 9 -11 and use its themes as a starting point for prayer for your church. Then ask everyone to pray in silence for the person on their right and then for the person on their left. Conclude by joining hands to say the Grace together.

Appropriate songs and hymns include the following found in Mission Praise 1 and 2:

13 As we are gathered
50 For I'm building a people of power
61 Go forth and tell
68 He is here, he is here
108 In the presence of your people
166 O for a closer walk with God
222 The King is among us
233 There's a quiet understanding
251 We are gathering together unto him
256 We really want to thank you, Lord
311 Blest be the tie that binds
369 God is building a house
412 I give you all the honour
421 I receive your love
429 I'm confident of this very thing
459 Jesus you are changing me
492 May the fragrance of Jesus
525 O the deep deep love of Jesus
626 When I look into your holiness
643 You are the one

More Learning Activities

1

Philippians 1.1 - 11

INTRODUCTION

This passage is:

- **about Labels (Paul calls his readers 'saints' and himself a 'slave');**
- **about two 'Big Gospel Words' ('grace' and 'peace');**
- **about Thanking God for other Christians' progress and gifts;**
- **about Asking God to give or do things for their brothers and sisters in Christ.**

The activities that follow try to come at these four ideas at a bit of an angle.

- ACTIVITY 1
  WHAT'S IT TO ME?
  (GRACE AND PEACE)

It is easy to let words like ***grace*** *and* ***peace*** *trip lightly off the tongue without really asking what they mean. This exercise tries to force us to think out what they might mean to different people. It's easier to work in pairs or even threes. Don't be afraid to doodle and experiment.*

Produce two acrostics.
Acrostics are sayings where the initial letter of a number of words taken together make up another word. The most famous is the early Christian sign 'Ichthus' (fish) which stands for Iesous Christos Theou Uios Soter (Jesus Christ God's Son Saviour).

Bible teachers explain Grace by saying it stands for "God's Riches At Christ's Expense".

You have to produce an acrostic for GRACE and PEACE. Your acrostic has to bring out what the words really mean. Talk about what each word means to you and then try to produce acrostics for the following people: a teenager; a child; a senior citizen; a non-Christian; yourself.

It was God
who Really
Arranged
your Conversion
Experience
And,
Life is Pretty
Excruciating
and Awful
but Christ
is in Everything

To make it a learning process the leader should read a theological dictionary definition, such as the ones below, after everyone has had a good try. Does this change anything?

"The New Testament emphasises that grace is the free gift of God and that it is not the outcome of man's deserving."

"'The biblical sense of peace is determined by the Hebrew word 'shalom' - 'well-being','harmony'...'the free growth of the soul'...'harmonious community'...'well-being manifested in every kind of good for man, bodily health, strengthening and security, happiness'...'The normal and proper condition of men in relationship with one another'. 'Unbroken union with the Father in the midst of adversity, which is the supreme gift of Jesus to the disciples'"

Now try to produce two calligrams on the two words Grace and Peace. Calligrams are words where the individual letters are pulled out of shape in such a way that the total shape of the words suggests its meaning. For example "SMILE" might look like this..

What is the shape of Grace and Peace?

When everyone has produced something talk about your efforts and explain what you were trying to get across. If this were a competition for a car sticker or a patch to go on a pair of jeans or a sampler for the wall of an Old Folk's Home which one would win the prize from your group?

ACTIVITY 2
THE PRAYER LETTER

This passage gives us an insight into Paul's prayer life and his prayer list. As he prays for the Philippians he follows this pattern:

A Label ("saints") - Paul is fond of labels, eg true yokefellow; son; brother; fellow soldier; messenger; minister to my needs; my joy; my crown.

A Thank You ("I thank God when I think of you because...")

A Conviction ("I am sure of this ...")

A Request ("It is my prayer that...")

Now it just so happens that we have discovered other prayers of St Paul. Following the pattern given above write the prayers of Paul for:

Your church (i.e. what **label** would you like Paul to address your church by, what does he **thank** God for, what is he absolutely **certain of**, etc?)

Another member of your housegroup:
(a label, a thank you, etc.)

Yourself (you may wish to keep this to yourself): (a label, a thank you, etc.)

We sometimes find it difficult to affirm one another publicly. Positive, strong labels might prove embarrassing both to give and to receive. Paul managed it though! This exercise could be undertaken lightheartedly but it would be better if the group could do it seriously and reflectively. It might be a good idea to turn 'the prayers' into real prayers for one another by distributing them around the group. Each person could then pray the prayer they find in front of themselves either aloud or, if that is tricky, during a period of silence.

ACTIVITY 3
PRAYER DOODLES

This is fairly lighthearted and might be a good exercise to begin with, Michel Quoist said "All life can become a prayer".

Doodle on a piece of paper. This might be your usual doodle or a special one for the occasion. Now turn the doodle into the subject of a prayer. For example,

"O Lord forgive me for rushing round in circles".

If it is difficult to think of a prayer (forgive, thank you, please, I praise you or...) ask your partner what your doodle suggests to them and work from there.

(Acknowledgments to Rev. Michael Ranyard for this idea.)

A Label

A Thank you

A Conviction

A Request

2

It's for him

Philippians 1.12-26

AIM To learn from Paul's example how to speak about Christ and live for him.

INTRODUCTION Just what place does Jesus have in our order of priorities? If we are honest for many of us he does not have the place he should. Paul could say unashamedly, "For me to live is Christ." Christ was at the centre of his life in all that he did. This was shown in the way he spoke about Christ to anyone and everyone - even imprisonment couldn't shut him up - he saw it as yet another opportunity to speak about Jesus. He didn't mind when others were speaking about Jesus out of rivalry (perhaps to be seen to 'outdo' Paul) - as long as Jesus was being talked about. Suffering for Jesus' sake didn't matter. His love for Jesus even overcame his human fear of death - it was just the gateway to a fuller knowledge of Jesus.

This week's "Begin Here" section is an evaluation exercise to help the group think about the place Jesus has in their conversation. The Bible study looks at several areas in which Jesus made a difference to Paul and his life and challenges us about our response in those areas. For the "Action" section you will need to photocopy the faces on **page 31**, later the book. They will help the group express their feelings about speaking about their faith to other people.

NOTES:

v.12: Paul's imprisonment might have held up the spread of the Gospel, as its most well-known preacher was put out of action. Instead it has given Paul new opportunities and given others encouragement to preach too.

v.13: The Praetorian Guard were the emperor's official guard, the only soldiers stationed in Rome itself - and so word has spread among them about the reason for Paul's imprisonment. This Greek word used here (praitorion) probably means the guard - though it was used of the Governor's palace in the provinces (the Authorized version translates it as "palace"); and so it may be an indication that this letter was written in an earlier imprisonment in the provinces - but this is unlikely. More probably it is a reference to Paul using the fact of his imprisonment as an excuse for explaining the Gospel to the guards around him!

v.14: The example of Paul's steadfastness has encouraged others to be bold in sharing the Gospel.

v.15: Some preached the Gospel out of love but some do it out of rivalry. As they were preaching Christ it is very unlikely Paul is speaking about false teachers, like the Judaizers with their half-Jewish Christianity, who opposed him in Galatia and elsewhere. The picture is, rather, of a group of Christians who had no kind of loyalty to Paul but instead resented his fame and so they had redoubled their efforts in evangelism to show how well the church could do without him.

v.16: "Put here" is a military term suggesting this is Paul's posting.

v.17: They are doing it "not sincerely" - that is with mixed motives in order to make Paul jealous.

v.18: Paul isn't accusing his rivals of preaching a Gospel they don't believe but of doing so from the wrong motives.

v.19: "This will turn out for my deliverance" is a quote from Job 13.16. The word for "deliverance" is "soterion" which is the word for "salvation". Paul is not saying he is confident he will be acquitted in a human court but that he will ultimately be vindicated.

v.20: The Greek word for "courage" means boldness or forthrightness in speaking about Christ. Paul's ambition is echoed by Lord Shaftesbury's words, "Perish all things, so that Christ be magnified!"

v.21: Paul's words "to die is gain" are not an expression of a "pie in the sky when you die" mentality which encourages you to endure hardship now because heaven will be better. It is because life with Christ now is so good that life beyond death, with no barriers between the Christian and his Saviour, is even better.

v.23: "Depart" is a euphemism for death.

v.24: Paul sees the pastoral needs of the Philippians which he would like to meet.

v.25: He feels he will be acquitted so that he can continue his work.

v.26: Paul speaks of exultant rejoicing when he comes to them. He uses the word "parousia" of his coming - the word he uses of the 'coming' of Jesus. It was the word for a king's welcome into a city.

SUNDAY EXTRA

Philippians 1.21 could be used as the key verse to show how Paul's life, lived with Christ, affected his attitude to -

1. Persecution (vv.12-14).
2. Preaching (vv.15-18).
3. Pastoral concern (vv.22-26).

or focus on the Christian's response to -

1. Life - "For me to live is Christ".
2. Death - "To die is gain".

For a Family Service talk focus on our response to persecution (even youngsters get picked on because of their Christian faith!) Use pictures of Paul in chains, a Roman soldier, Paul on trial, to talk about Paul's response - contrasting this with our witness at school or work and among friends and neighbours.

Interview someone who has faced opposition because of their Christian faith or focus on Christians facing persecution in other countries.

Pray for those facing persecution, those preaching the Gospel, the dying. Include thanksgiving that, "For me to live is Christ, to die is gain".
Church Family Worship Sections 28 and 31 may be helpful. Further hymns and songs are listed in the "Worship and Prayer" section.

2 Group Sheet

It's for him

Philippians 1.12-26

AIM To learn from Paul's example how to speak about Christ and live for him.

BEGIN HERE

Number in order the things you talk most about.

Work ___

Sport ___

Family ___

Fashions ___

Food ___

House ___

Hobbies ___

Share your results in pairs. Where in that list would you place your faith - how much do you talk about that? Share again in pairs.

BIBLE STUDY

READ PHILIPPIANS 1. 12-26

Witness

How did Paul help to make the Good News known?

How did Paul's imprisonment encourage others to share their faith?

How is the Good News made known today?

What encourages us to share it?

Motives

How did Paul react to others' motives for sharing the Good News? (vv 15-18)

Are there ways in which we are critical of the work of other Christians?

How does Paul's example challenge such attitudes?

Suffering

What was Paul's attitude to his imprisonment?

How can Paul's assurance reassure us in the difficult situations we face?

Life and Death

How did Paul view the future? (vv.19-26).

Why did he have that confidence?

ACTION

Pick out three faces from those on the sheet which express your reaction to the suggestion that you get involved in telling other people about the Lord. Share in groups of three or four which faces you have chosen and why you react that way. How can we deal with some of the adverse reactions we have? Can we help each other? How?

ADDITIONAL QUESTIONS

Witness

- Paul used the situation he was in as an opportunity for witness.
  What situations can provide opportunities for us to speak about Jesus?
- What are the contrasts between the way we talk about Christ and the way Paul did?
  Why is there a difference?

Motives

- What are the right motives for sharing the Good News about Jesus?
- In what ways can we do Christian work out of a partisan spirit?

Suffering

- Look at the example of Paul's experience of suffering (see 2 Corinthians 11.23-29).
  How do we experience suffering?
- How can difficult situations serve to "advance the Gospel"?

Life and Death

- How do we feel about death? Do we look forward to it and life with Christ beyond it?
  If not, why are we so earth-bound in our thinking?
- Share what it means for you to say "to live is Christ".
- Why did Paul want to live? What goals for Christian service do we have?

WORSHIP AND PRAYER

Pray a meditative prayer aimed at focussing Christ's presence into every part of our lives. It could have sections beginning, for example, "When I am at work and ...." or "When I am not well and ...." After each section everyone joins in the words "For me to live is Christ. To die is gain". Alternatively, all or some of "St. Patrick's Breastplate" (the hymn "I bind into myself today") could be read as a meditation - especially the section "Christ be with me".

Pray for the witness of your church and its members and for those suffering because of their faith in Christ.

Suitable songs in Mission Praise 1 and 2 include:

29	Christ is the answer
41	Do not be afraid
45	Father, I place into your hands
49	Fight the good fight
60	God forgave my sin
76	How firm a foundation
84	I have decided to follow Jesus
95	I trust in thee, O Lord
100	I'm not ashamed to own my Lord
106	In heavenly love abiding
196	Restore, O Lord
249	O soul, are you weary and troubled
303	As the deer pants for the water
409	I do not know what lies ahead
415	I live, I live because he is risen
445	It is no longer I that liveth
495	My life is yours, O Lord
531	One shall tell another
543	Rejoice! rejoice!
579	In heavenly armour

More Learning Activities

2 Philippians 1.12-26

INTRODUCTION

This passage is about Paul's reaction to the difficulties of the present (vv 12-18) and the uncertainties of the future (vv 19-26). As we read between his lines we can see certain pressures which threaten to crush him but also his convictions and his priorities. The exercises try to force us to apply Paul's perspective on what he experienced to our own world.

- ACTIVITY 1
  RENT A SERMON

You are sitting quietly at home when the phone rings. It's the Vicar. "I'm awfully sorry to bother you," he says, "I've got to go to an urgent commination service and I'll be away a day or two. Can you do me a favour?"

"Of course," you reply. "Well, I need a sermon for later in the week. I won't have time to prepare it. If I drop the headings in do you think you could fill it in for me. Then I can just preach it when I get back." You agree to help, perhaps unwisely. That evening the outline drops on to the door-mat. There's a note attached.

> Dear................, Thanks for your help. I've sorted out the headings. Paul's pressures, Paul's presuppositions, Paul's priorities. By the way did I tell you I'm giving this talk to a group of Christian businessmen/ the sixth form at the Comprehensive school/ an evangelistic housegroup evening at the Jacksons'/ the Young Mums.

Choose one of these audiences. Your task (with a partner) is to get a preachable outline ready for the Vicar. Fortunately you've heard the Vicar preach many times and know his style. So...

Read (and re-read) the passage. Think up some rather more exciting headings to replace pressures, presuppositions and priorities - I ask you! Customise the pictures and illustrations so that they are relevant to the listeners. Complete the following outline:

> **HEADING 1**
> PAUL'S PRESSURES
> (NEW HEADING)
>
> **One picture or image or analogy.** "My dear friends it is a little bit like..."
>
> **One real situation to illustrate the main point** of this section from a modern standpoint. "I am reminded of an incident/person/ film/something I was reading only the other day/something I over-heard in the supermarket, etc..."
>
> **One objection**, "But some of you might be thinking,'That's all very well ,Vicar, but what about...?"

Repeat this pattern for the other two headings,

HEADING 2
PAUL'S PRESUPPOSITIONS

HEADING 3
PAUL'S PRIORITIES

ACTIVITY 2
OPPORTUNITY KNOCKS

What is so exciting, inspiring, maddening about Paul is the way in which what would lead most people to despair and whingeing leads him to see Christ at work. "I want you to know that the things that have happened to me have really served to advance the gospel".

Things which might seem to be disasters do often by the grace of God enhance our lives and reveal his activity.

*This exercise can be played lightheartedly **and** seriously. And perhaps it should be both.*

Make a set of cards or slips of paper and label them Disaster, Excuse, Opportunity until they are all used up. You need a few more than the number expected for the group.

Deal out the cards marked Disaster/Excuse/Opportunity.

One person with a **Disaster** card invents and briefly describes a disaster.

The **Excuses** group then demonstrate how this disaster has had terrible effects on the person's life and use it as an excuse for not doing X,Y,Z, or behaving in way A,B,C.

Then the **Opportunity** group show how strange to relate and against what you would expect the disaster turned out to have positive consequences after all.

Do a few for fun, e.g. "As you are getting ready to leave for Church on Sunday morning you accidently leave the sink tap running - and plug it in."

"The visiting preacher at the Prison falls flat on his face as he walks up the steps to give a talk to the prisoners."

Remember to reallocate Disaster, Excuses and Opportunity cards each time.

Now do some for Paul based on this passage.

> "With Paul in jail other Christians take on the preaching - some with very questionable motives."
>
> "It becomes clear to Paul that he may have to face the death sentence."

In these cases we know what the Opportunity group will say because Paul got there first. But the Excuses group can have a field day if they use their imaginations.

Now do some others, some (most) fictional, but perhaps if the mood gets more serious some might be real disasters...

3

United we stand

Philippians 1.27 - 2.11

AIM To see that Christ-like humility and service are the key to a united witness to others.

INTRODUCTION

We regularly quote things out of their original context - but often they lose something of their original meaning in the process. That's true of the words of Philippians 2.5-11, which the Alternative Service Book uses as the canticle "The Song of Christ's Glory". The passage is an incredibly beautiful and moving description of the way Christ, out of love for us, humbled himself in becoming man but was then exalted by God. It may have been a quotation from a hymn already in existence which Paul used here, which gives us some justification for using it that way. Nevertheless, in its context it is not an abstract hymn of praise but it has a very practical purpose. Christ's example is used to encourage Christians to show humility in their relationships with one another and to have a willingness to serve. If they follow that example, says Paul, they will be able to overcome their divisions and so work and witness for Christ in a united way, which will deal with the opposition they face. This pathway of humility and service is the opposite to that which the world takes.

Our study begins by focussing on the value of unity and then looks at the sort of unity we should display and the Christ-like path of humble service. The "Action" section aims to crystallize ideas about the service we should be undertaking and/or the service in which we are currently involved.

NOTES

Chapter 1:

v.27: There are three separate metaphors lying behind the words of this verse. "Let your manner of life be" translates the Greek word "politeuesthai" which means "behave as citizens". By their behaviour Christians are to show their allegiance to Christ and his kingdom. A military picture is conjured up by words about "standing firm" - like an army ready to repulse the attack. While the last phrase about striving or contending side by side relates to the picture of athletes in the stadium (the Greek is "synathlountes"). They are not just to defend the Gospel but to strive to spread it.

v.28: "Frightened" is a descriptive word which pictures horses being stampeded. The unity of the Church in the face of opposition is to act as proof to their opponents that God is on their side. This has eternal consequences. For the believer there is the promise of salvation, for the unbeliever there is future judgement. (This does not, of course, rule out some of their enemies changing sides and so experiencing salvation!)

v.29: Suffering for Christ's sake is seen as a privilege (see 2 Corinthians 12.10, Philippians 3.8-10, 1 Peter 4.12-16).

v.30: Acts 16.19-40 tells of the opposition Paul faced in Philippi and which they saw when their church was founded. Now they hear about his imprisonment too. The opposition they face is part of the same ongoing battle.

Chapter 2:

v.1: It is possible (as the New International Version does) to take all the references in this verse as being to the things we receive from Christ or the Spirit - encouragement, love, fellowship with God, compassion. It is also possible that they refer to our common life "in Christ" and so refer to encouragement and love received from others, the fellowship with one another in the Spirit, the compassion Christians have for each other (as the New English Bible does). In view of the fact that this is an encouragement to unity the latter sense might seem more likely but, on the other hand, our common experience of Christ's love etc. is a uniting factor (Paul uses that as an argument for unity in Ephesians 4.4-6). Take your pick - it might mean either or both!

v.2: Paul is not asking them to be of "one mind" in an intellectual sense. The New International Version is closer in speaking of "purpose".

v.3: Humility was despised in the ancient world. It is only because of Jesus' teaching and example that it became seen as a virtue.

v.4: Concern for others comes before concern for self.

v.5: Those who belong to Christ should reflect his example in their life together.

v.6: This verse is best understood as a contrast with Adam. He did not have the right to equality with God but grasped at that dignity. Jesus who had that status was willing to let it go.

v.7: It has sometimes been suggested that Christ "emptying" himself meant laying aside all the attributes of deity such as omniscience and omnipotence. In fact the verse says nothing about such things but speaks of him laying aside the status and rights of Godhead and taking instead those of the servant. He became fully man, sharing in all our humanity.

v.8: Jesus' obedience to the Father was shown in his willingness not only to die, but to die on a cross - the symbol of rejection by God and man. He did it to fulfill God's plan to reconcile us to himself.

v.9: The heavenly Christ returns to the glory he had before - but he does so now as a man. He is given the highest honour in "the name above all names". The "name" he is given is not "Jesus" by which he was known in his lifetime but that of "Lord".

vv.10-11: Isaiah 45.23 is quoted here - words applied to God are now applied to Jesus in recognition of his true nature and status. The whole of creation has to recognize his lordship. "Jesus is Lord" was the basic confession of the early church. (See Romans 10.9 and 1 Corinthians 12.3). Christ's Lordship is not in competition with that of the Father but brings glory to him.

SUNDAY EXTRA

This week you could either link up with the theme of the Bible study and focus on the pursuit of unity in the church's life or look more fully at the picture of Christ in 2.5-11.

A sermon could look at aspects of Unity -

1. The necessity (1.27-30)
2. The basis (2.1-2)
3. The practice (2.3-4)
4. The example (2.5-11)

C.S. Lewis's picture of the diver - ("Miracles" p.115-116 Fontana edition) could form a focus for a sermon on Jesus - showing the depths to which he was willing to go in order to save us (emphasize the stages outlined in verses 5-9) and the greatness of his position now, and the need to acknowledge him not only as Saviour but as Lord. C.S.Lewis writes, "One may think of a diver, first reducing himself to nakedness, then glancing in mid-air, then gone with a splash, vanished, rushing down through green and warm water into black and cold water, down through increasing pressure into the death-like region of ooze and slime and old decay; then up again, back to colour and light, his lungs almost bursting, till suddenly he breaks the surface again, holding in his hand the precious thing that he went down to recover. He and it are both coloured now that they have come up into the light: down below, where it lay colourless in the dark, he lost his colour too."

Michael Botting's book "Teaching the Families" (pages 186-188) had a very good talk for a Family Service based on Philippians 2.5-11. The speaker outlines verses 5-8 while removing his robes to reveal a dustman's outfit and then collects in a dustbin people's sins (labels previously distributed) and explains how Jesus dealt with these. He then explains verses 9-11 while dressing in the robes of a king.

Church Family Worship sections 11 and 19 will be helpful. Prayers for the church's unity, as well as praise of Christ for his humility and his glory would be appropriate. Hymns and songs are listed overleaf.

Group Sheet 3

United we stand

Philippians 1.27 - 2.11

AIM To see that Christ-like humility and service are the key to a united witness to others.

BEGIN HERE
"United we stand, divided we fall," goes the saying.
List examples which prove the truth of that, either from history or your own experience.

BIBLE STUDY
READ PHILIPPIANS 1.27 - 2.11

Unity
Why is Paul keen that Christians should be united? (1.27-30). What are the things which should prompt our oneness? (2.1-2). How do we receive encouragement from the fellowship of God's people? What evidence can you see in your church of people being: like-minded? having the "same love"? being one in spirit and purpose?

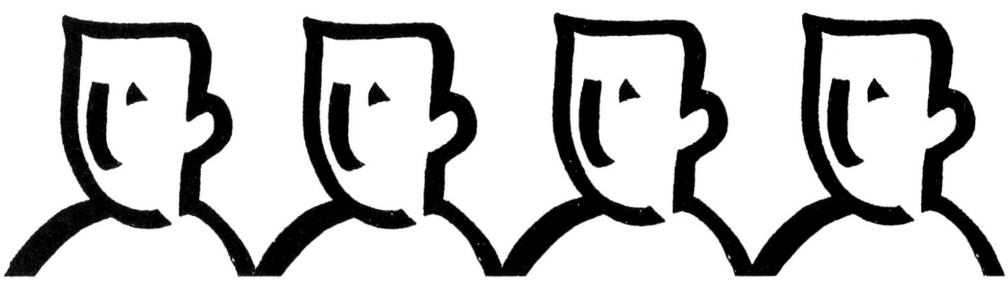

Humility
What does Paul teach about the nature of true humility? How does this differ from the attitudes of those around us? How might selfish ambition or vain conceit show itself in a Christian today? What does Jesus' example demonstrate about humility and service? (2.5-11). Why did he do all this? How can we put others first in the way we live our lives?

ACTION
Are there practical ways in which you should be serving others?
Share any areas of service which you are finding difficult and in which you would appreciate encouragement and prayer.

ADDITIONAL QUESTIONS

Unity

- Why is it important that our lives should be "worthy of the Gospel of Christ"? (1.27) What things in the way we live can demonstrate to others that we believe in Christ?
- What is the effect of our unity on those who oppose us? (1.28).
- Is suffering for the faith part of the experience of all Christians? (1.29-30)
- How would the Philippians' unity bring joy to Paul? (2.2) Are there examples you can share of the way others have encouraged you through their Christian living?

Humility

- How do we count others "better than ourselves" when we feel, in all honesty, that we are better than them? (2.3)
  Should we have a low estimate of ourselves and our abilities?
- Should we look to our own interests? (2.4)
- What does Paul's picture of Christ (2.5-11) teach us about Christ's true nature? About his incarnation? About his position now? About his future position?

PRAYER AND WORSHIP

Follow the study by prayer in small groups about our areas of service for Christ.
Use 2.5-11 as a meditation, allowing time for reflection after each phrase.
Follow this with a time of praise.

Songs and hymns from Mission Praise could include:

5	All hail the power of Jesus' name
15	At the name of Jesus
21	Bind us together, Lord
39	Crown him with many crowns
69	He is Lord
71	His name is higher
124	Jesus stand among us
137	Let there be love
139	Lift high the cross
204	Sing alleluia
224	The Lord is a great and mighty king
283	A new commandment
301	An army of ordinary people
361	From heaven you came
407	I confess that Jesus Christ is Lord
446	Jesus at your name we bow the knee
448	Jesus has sat down
457	Jesus put this song into our hearts
493	Meekness and majesty
644	You laid aside your majesty.

More Learning Activities

3 Philippians 1.27 - 2.11

INTRODUCTION

The following four exercises try to pick up the three themes of the section - the unity of the church, the conflict and struggle which Christians are engaged in and 'let this mind be in you which was in Christ Jesus...'.

- ACTIVITY 1
  SCREWTAPE ENTERPRISES

There are a number of words which highlight the importance of unity among Christians.

in one spirit;
with one mind;
striving together;
of the same mind;
having the same love;
in full accord;
of one mind;
not through selfish ambition or vain conceit

Divide the group into threes or fours. Each smaller group is a firm of 'Disunity Consultants'. Choose a name or make one up: eg Unman, Screwtape and Withering; Ripoff; Grabbit and Run; Noisome Enterprises; Strifecon. The Client (Darkness Limited) is a multi-national company with outlets and operatives all over the world. They approached you for proposals for a cast- iron, guaranteed package for sowing division, strife and disunity into St Accord's (a church not unlike your own). The brief is simple.

Aim: to produce maximum disunity, backbiting, conflict and strife within a period of twelve months.

Method: invisible infiltration.

Components: you are allowed to insert into the life of the church ...

1 book (real or imaginary) onto the parish bookstall.
Please give exact title and short synopsis of contents

1 event which will take place during the year as part of the church's programme

1 item on the PCC agenda
(no-one will quite know how it got there - but this happens quite often!)

1 "good cause" to be supported by money from the parish

1 remark to be overheard in a public place and suitable to be spread like wildfire

1 disaster to befall the church
(but be careful - the Enemy has a way of turning these into triumphs)

1 "tremendous success" which will produce long term resentment

1 paragraph in the church magazine

After a suitable time for preparation each firm will give a short presentation explaining and extolling the merits of their particular package; how they have handled the items in the above list, what effect they expect each to have and what they predict to be the state of the church in a year's time. A decision then needs to be made by the leader or by a group vote as to the package most likely to succeed.

After this activity groups may well feel a little negative. After all they've spent the evening trying to destroy a church. It is essential that time should be spent discussing the experience. The Leader should help the members to analyse the different kinds of "triggers" and "flashpoints" which lead to division. How realistic were the various suggestions? What are the particular sins that lie at the root of disunity? How can we put Paul's exhortations into practice? What positive strategies can members suggest to counter the campaign which has been mounted against St Accord's?

● ACTIVITY 2
THE SINGLEMINDED GAME

"Let each of you look not only to his own interests but also to the interests of others" (2.4). Strictly speaking this is impossible. It only becomes possible when the body of Christ is acting as one body.

A fairly light-hearted, though perhaps revealing, exercise is as follows:

You will need a large piece of paper. Two people both hold one felt tip pen. Without speaking they both draw whatever you set them ... a circle, a giraffe, their ideal house. Afterwards the group discusses the different ways in which the problems posed by this situation were resolved. What parallels can be drawn with Christians trying to live and work together?

The source for this exercise is Ron Wiener, "Running Staff Training Groups", Leeds Polytechnic.

● ACTIVITY 3
CATCH A FALLING STAR

Think of an experience that you have had which corresponds to the *striving* part of the passage. It might be a time when you had to *stand firm* and not waver; or *strive* to achieve an important but difficult goal; perhaps you were *frightened* or facing *opposition*; maybe the experience involved *suffering* or *struggle*. New aspects of the experience come to light when we have to force it into a different form.

So try to draw that experience, as a pattern.

And use a colour, or colours, to express what it felt like.

Is there an image or picture which will capture the feeling of the experience? Maybe it was like an animal or an object or something in the natural world. Perhaps you can draw it as a diagram.

What background music is playing as you think of the experience?

People often send cards to those who are going through a difficult time. Unfortunately the cards don't always hit the right note. As you think back, what card would you have liked to receive? Sketch out the design (it doesn't matter how roughly) and put a motto or verse or comment inside.

Ideally, at the end, people should share what they have done with another person.

● ACTIVITY 4
THE JESUS VISIT

Divide the group into smaller groups of three or four.

Jesus is coming to visit your church and area. Your task is to plan an itinerary for him. He will be in the area for a whole day. You need to specify an exact timetable (eg. 9.30 meet X at Y; 10.15 move on to Z by route 'A' etc). Where he goes; who he meets and talks to; what his programme is; which parts of your church and/or area he sees (and which you do not take him to) are all entirely up to you. Money is no object. You may lay on any programme you wish.

After the planning stage the groups present their proposed itineraries.

The value of the exercise will lie in the discussion that follows. Groups need to explain why they created the programmes they did. At some point the leader needs to draw their attention to Phil. 2.4-11 and raise questions about how far the various schedules try to reflect "the mind of Christ".

Did Jesus see all the 'right people?
What areas of the church and town were thought appropriate?
What proportion of time was spent with the church as opposed to the town?
Did the Christians keep him to themselves or did they display the same "emptying" and "self-giving" as Jesus did?
What did the schedules reveal about the picture we have of "the mind of Christ"?

The idea for this exercise is taken from Jim Belben and Trevor Cooper, "Everyone's A Winner", Bible Society. (1987)

4

That's encouraging

Philippians 2.12-30

AIM To learn ways of giving encouragement to one another both practically and spiritually.

INTRODUCTION

"That was a lovely sermon, Vicar!" says the lady at the church door. The problem with "lovely sermons" is that they give you a warm glow inside and then are forgotten about, instead of being acted on. It is very easy to respond like that to the wonderful words in chapter 2.5-11 which we looked at last week. They are tremendously inspiring and uplifting - but it mustn't end there. Paul has a nasty habit of turning doctrine into practice! His letters are full of inspiring passages followed by the word "therefore" leading into an outline of the practical consequences of our beliefs. Chapter 2.12 is such a turning point - the self-sacrificing humility of Christ should affect our relationships and be seen in our care for one another.

We learn much from the examples of others and so this week's study takes the form of four character studies. Paul provides us in these verses with pen-portraits of his colleague Timothy and of Epaphroditus, the Philippians' messenger to him. The passage also contains a picture of the sort of people Paul wanted the Philippians to be and his words reveal his own care for his fellow-Christians and his relationships with them - as pastor, as "father in Christ", as fellow-worker. It may take too long to look at all four in the time you have available. Either omit one or more of the studies or divide them between 2 groups and have a report back session at the end.

NOTES

v.12 "Therefore" links the example of Christ and its application in the life of Christians. As Christ obeyed the Father so too they must obey God's will. Paul has seen their obedience in his times with them and heard of it since, but his absence (which may be permanent if he is put to death) should not be an excuse for going their own way but instead should be a spur to further obedience. Paul is not saying here that they are saved by virtue of any good which they do - the principle of salvation by faith in Christ is spelt out clearly in all his letters. However, we must work out in practice, in our relationships with one another, what it means to be a saved people - and do so in a spirit of reverence for God.

v.13 God's work within us enables us both to want God's will and to do it.

v.14 Paul is probably thinking here of the Israelites who grumbled against God - verse 15 quotes Deuteronomy 32.5 where Moses speaks about the disobedient Israelites as a "crooked and perverse generation".

v.15 Like the unbelieving Jews the world around has rejected God. In contrast the Christians are to be light-bearers (compare Matthew 5.14-16) by their blameless behaviour.

v.16 This verse is translated differently in the various versions of the Bible. It may mean that they are to "hold fast" to the Gospel or that they are to "hold out" or "proffer" the Gospel. The latter would be more in keeping with the picture of the Christian bringing light in verse 15. Paul wants to know that on judgement day his work has been worthwhile - that he has played his part in building the church (see 1 Corinthians 3.12-15).

v.17 The picture is one of sacrifice. Paul sees his blood shed in martyrdom as being like the drink-offering which was poured out as an accompaniment to a sacrificial offering. The offering here is that of the Philippians who offer themselves and all they have to God because of their faith in him (compare Romans 12.1).

v.18 Even facing death Paul's reaction is that of joy.

v.19 Paul doesn't make his plans independently, he does so in fellowship with Jesus.

v.20 Timothy had been with Paul when the church in Philippi was founded (see Acts 16) and so shared Paul's concern for the Christians there.

v.21 Perhaps Paul had asked others to undertake the mission but they had all made their excuses on what Paul sees as rather unworthy grounds or, maybe, Paul sees there is no one else whom he could send who would have the unselfish devotion that Timothy had.

v.22 Just as a father taught his son all there was to know about his trade, so Paul had taught Timothy and shaped his life and ministry as he travelled and worked with Paul.

vv.23-24 Paul is awaiting the outcome of his trial. He hopes to be acquitted and so be able to visit them too.

v.25 This is the only place where we read of Epaphroditus but obviously Paul has a great affection for him. He trusts him as someone who can be counted as a fellow-worker and soldier in Christ's cause. He had been sent by the Philippians to bring their gifts and to help look after Paul.

vv.26-28 The simple answer to the problem of the Philippians and Epaphroditus worrying about each other was to send him back home and so put an end to their worries.

vv.29-30 Paul wants to avoid any misunderstanding there might be over Epaphroditus' return. It was not because he had failed in his commission to serve Paul. Indeed he had risked his life to do so, completing his journey while he was ill, it would seem.

SUNDAY EXTRA

There are a number of themes in this week's passage which could form the focus for the sermon.

- Our responsibility to **work out** our salvation in our Christian living, while God is at **work in** us.
- Our lifestyle in the world (vv.14-18).
- Character studies of Timothy and Epaphroditus.

For a Family Service, Church Leadership Pack 9 had a drama about "The Grumbling Community" based on the Exodus story, which could be linked to the references in vv.14-15. Alternatively, tell Timothy's life-story, with appropriate pictures, - his upbringing learning from the Scriptures, leaving home to work with Paul, some of the places to which he went, the problems he had to overcome, (such as his shyness) in order to lead a church, his dedication to the service of Christ.

Church Family Worship sections 26 and 27 might be helpful. Prayers for those called to full-time Christian ministry and for the witness of our lives would be appropriate.

4 Group Sheet

That's encouraging

Philippians 2.12-30

AIM To learn ways of giving encouragement to one another both practically and spiritually.

BEGIN HERE
Ask everyone to think of a person who either was greatly involved in their becoming a Christian or who has helped them grow in the Christian faith and to write down things about that person which helped them. In small groups share those characteristics.

BIBLE STUDY
READ PHILIPPIANS 2.12-30

The Philippians
How does Paul expect the Philippian Christians to be living their lives? What will help them?
How can we "shine" in the world today? (vv.12-18). How had they shown their concern for Paul? How can you and your church show concern for others? (vv.25-9, see also 4.14-18).

Timothy
What sort of person was Timothy? (vv.19-23). Why are people like him important in the life of the church? In what ways do our interests come before those of Christ? Why is this?

Epaphroditus
How had Epaphroditus shown his commitment to Christ? and to his fellow Christians? (vv.25-29). How do we react to hardships- do we give in to self-pity and moan and groan?

Paul
What sort of relationships did Paul have with the Philippians, with Timothy and with Epaphroditus? Why are there differences? How do we see this variety of relationships in the church today? What do these verses show us about Paul as a pastor?

ACTION
Are there ways in which we should be meeting the needs of others - in our church, in other churches? Are there people to whom we should be giving encouragement? Try to be specific.

ADDITIONAL QUESTIONS

The Philippians

- How do we maintain the right balance in our thinking about the Christian life between the effort we must make and our dependence upon God's help and enabling?
- Does it help us to feel we are accountable to someone, as the Philippians were to Paul (v.12) or should we be able to be trusted to get on with things by ourselves?
- What should be the differences in life-style between us and the non-Christians around us? (vv.14-16).

Timothy

- You might like to look at Timothy in more depth by looking up these verses. Acts 16.1-3, 1 Corinthians 16.10-11, 1 Timothy 4.14, Hebrews 13.23, Romans 16.21, 2 Corinthians 1.19, 2 Timothy 1.4-8, 1 Timothy 1.18 and 2 Timothy 2.22.
- What were his strengths? What were his weaknesses? Write a reference for Timothy who is one of your group and wants to join Paul's missionary team.

Epaphroditus

- What do the various descriptions of Epaphroditus in verse 25 tell us about the variety of roles and relationships one Christian can have? How do the group's members have such a variety of roles? Are there tensions between the differing roles?
- How do verses 26-30 illustrate some of the varying ways we react to illness?
- Should Epaphroditus have been so worried?

Paul

- What does this passage show about Paul's dependence on the support of other Christians?
- How well do we support our spiritual leaders such as our minister (or even our bishop)?
- What qualities do we look for in
  - brothers
  - fellow-workers
  - fellow-soldiers

  Are these qualities to be found in our church/work-force/army? Are there any qualities which are lacking or weak? How can we improve?

WORSHIP AND PRAYER

In your worship this week you might like to lead prayers of thanksgiving for the spiritual "parents" who led us to faith and prayer for spiritual children whom we have helped, allowing opportunity for group members to mention people by name. Personal relationships within the church should be the major focus of intercession.

Possible songs and hymns in Mission Praise include -

13	As we are gathered	274	Who is on the Lord's side
21	Bind us together, Lord	283	A new commandment
27	Christ is made the sure foundation	288	All earth was dark
45	Father, I place into your hands	301	An army of ordinary people
51	For all the saints	349	Father make us one
124	Jesus stand among us	435	In Christ there is no East or West
148	Lord, speak to me	457	Jesus put this song into our hearts
153	Make me a channel of your peace	466	Let saints on earth in concert sing
254	We are one in the Spirit	631	Wind, wind blow on me
256	We really want to thank you, Lord	643	You are the vine

More Learning Activitie

4 Philippians 2.12-30

INTRODUCTION

2:12-18 are a mixture of verses unpacking the meaning of "work out your own salvation"; 2: 19-30 looks in detail at two of Paul's companions and helpers. The exercises reflect this division.

● ACTIVITY 1
THE VISUAL BIBLE

The task here is to produce a wall display for part of a Visual Bible designed to make the message of the Bible intelligible, attractive and relevant to the present generation. Each small group (pairs? threes?) works with felt-tips, scissors, paste, magazine colour supplements and newspapers to communicate Paul's message in vv12-18.

The result should be:-

intelligible - that is, it should actually say what Paul is saying without grossly distorting his message;

attractive - that is, people should want to cross the road to look at it;

relevant - that is, it should try to suggest what Paul's words might mean for us today. *Encourage the groups not to be afraid of "Private Eye" speech and "thinks" bubbles, to use colour, pattern and 3D effects, to explore montage, collage and other ways of presenting modern equivalents of ancient images ('poured out like a libation on the sacrificial altar of your faith' etc.).*

● ACTIVITY 2
A MODERN TRANSLATION

This is a written version of the above exercise. The task is simply to translate (ie freely paraphrase) Paul's words. However, the paraphrase is aimed at a particular recipient of the group's choice, who might be a new Christian, your grandmother, an ordinand, someone you work with in the church or whoever. The golden rule is that you may not use any of the words in the passage in your translation (obviously this doesn't refer to 'the'. 'and','but' etc). Write the passage as you would say it; make it clear; say it directly and with force.

● ACTIVITY 3
THE JOB INTERVIEW

Advertisements for church workers usually ask for a cross between St Paul, Mother Teresa and the Archangel Gabriel.

Imagine your church is looking for a pastoral and evangelistic assistant with special responsibility for liaison with neighbouring Christian communities. The job is described in The Church Times as follows:

> Wanted for St Faith's Church, Wythomonley a pastoral assistant to work with the Vicar. The person appointed will be someone of some experience able to meet the pastoral needs of a fast-growing congregation and to help in evangelism in a diverse parish with both council and private housing. The person appointed will also be responsible for developing a network of mutual support with other churches in the locality.

Only two candidates apply - Timothy and Epaphroditus.

Divide the group in half. One half represents Timothy and the other Epaphroditus. Each group writes a Curriculum Vitae for its applicant based partly on the information contained in Philippians and Acts and partly on the vivid corporate imagination. The CV should not contain anything which is actually contradicted by the biblical passage.

Next, each group writes the reference which Paul has submitted in support of each candidate.

An interviewing panel (four people?) is formed from members of the group and two brave spirits volunteer to play Timothy and Epaphroditus and be interviewed for the job.

Discussion follows and the group makes an appointment.

It's for him

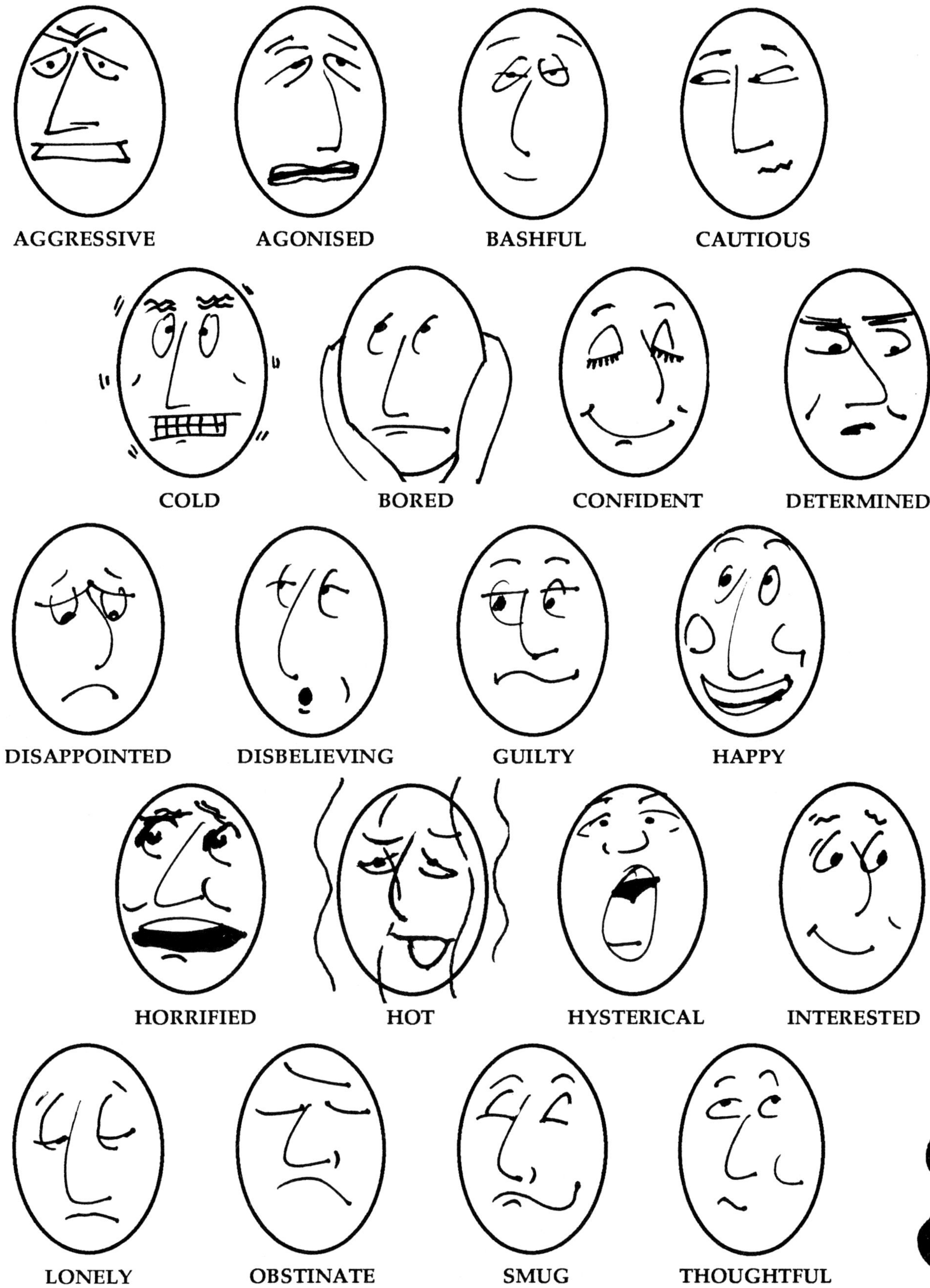

This series is adapted from Games Without Frontiers by Pip Wilson

5

Gains & losses

Philippians 3.1-21

AIM To renew the vision of that whole-hearted commitment to Christ which is essential if we are to experience to the full the joy of Christian living.

INTRODUCTION

The student aiming for a good degree, the young man starting out in business, the mum bringing up a family have all got goals for which to work. They will work hard and sacrifice much in order to achieve those goals. This week's study presents a challenge to us as Christians about our aims and goals. The first half of the passage takes us to the heart of the Gospel when we are reminded that we cannot put our trust in our own pedigree or good living as the basis for our acceptance by God - indeed we have to totally renounce any such attempts to earn our salvation by our good living. We have to put our trust in Christ alone in order to receive his righteousness, which enables us to stand before God without fear of condemnation. As we trust in him we also gain so much more - his life at work within us and the hope of eternal life too.

If we are to enjoy this life with Christ to the full, however, we need to give Christ the first place in our lives. We must allow him to determine the shape of our lives. We must live to please him. It is very easy for other things to become more important to us than Christ and so this week's study challenges us to weigh up the gains and losses of the Christian life and to reassess our goals.

The "Begin Here" section challenges people to think what matters most to them. The Study looks first at the losses, then at the gains involved in the Christian life while the "Action" section challenges us about our goals and how well we are achieving them.

NOTES

v.2-3 Paul uses three descriptions for the Jews who insisted on the practice of circumcision and the keeping of the law, arguing instead that Christians are the true people of God. "Dogs" was a name the Jews used of the Gentiles whom they despised - here Paul uses it of them; those who pride themselves on their good works are called workers of evil, while those who pride themselves on their circumcision (peritome in Greek) are called those who mutilate the body (katatome). The truly circumcised people of God are the Christians whose religion is an inward and spiritual one instead of an outward and ritual one, who put their trust in Christ instead of in their own ability to save themselves.

vv.4-6 Paul outlines the ways he could beat the Jews at their own game - if he wanted to do so. He was circumcised on the eighth day as the law required, of pure Jewish blood, from the tribe of Benjamin which had remained faithful to the family of David, a true Hebrew-speaking Jew. His concern for the law led him to be one of the small group of Pharisees, his zeal led him to oppose Christians. Outwardly he had kept the law (elsewhere he speaks of the inward conflict of which he was aware).

v.7 Because of all that Christ means to him Paul is willing to count all his former privileges and achievements as loss. He treats them as a liability because any boasting in them gets in the way of his knowledge of Christ.

v.8 Paul speaks of the relationship which he has with Christ far outweighing the things he must put aside. Paul's rejection of his law- keeping good record is so firm he describes it as rubbish to be thrown out. Christ alone is the source of our salvation.

v.9 In a few words here Paul summarizes the teaching at the heart of his letters to Rome and Galatia. In order to be declared righteous by God and acquitted on judgement day we need to acknowledge that our own good deeds will never make us good enough. We need to admit that we cannot earn God's approval but can only accept, by trust in Christ, his offer of forgiveness which brings us a new status of righteousness before God.

vv.10-11 The Christian finds new forces at work in his life - the presence of Christ's resurrection new life, which changes us within, enabling us to bear suffering for Christ's sake, letting our old life die so that the new may live. These things we experience now - but we can look forward to their final fulfilment when we are raised to life with Christ.

vv.12-14 Paul reminds us that all these tremendous gains should not lead to us resting on our laurels and boasting of a new status. He uses a new picture - that of the race to remind us to put all our effort into living this life with Christ. We are not instantly made perfect but our lives are constantly being transformed, until the day when Christ brings that process to completion at his second coming and we enjoy the life of heaven. Paul reminds us that this is in response to Christ's initiative - his making us his own, his call to the glory of eternal life.

vv.15-16 Paul argues that the mark of true Christian maturity is an awareness of the need to keep on making progress in the Christian life. We can never claim to have "arrived" or be "perfect". He expects others to agree with him on this - but if they don't then God can give them the insight to see the truth of what he is saying.

v.17 Paul often urges people to imitate him - to live the life of faith in the way which he has done. In doing so they will be imitating the Christ whom Paul followed. If Paul was not present with them they could follow the example of those who lived the same sort of life that he did. It is helpful to see the way others faithfully live out the Christian life.

vv.18-19 There are those who claim to be Christian, whose example they are not to follow. Their beliefs and behaviour are sub-Christian. In the early church, as today, there are those who seek to water down Christian faith and remove the "offensive elements", such as the cross, or who argue that Christian freedom permits a pursuit of pleasure and even immorality.

vv.20-21 Paul speaks of Christians as members of a heavenly kingdom - a colony of heaven on earth. From heaven we expect Jesus to come again and at his coming he will transform us, so that we receive those bodies which are fitted to the life of heaven. (See 1 Corinthians 15.49-53).

SUNDAY EXTRA

Once again there are several themes which could form the basis for this week's worship. From the first half of the passage you can explore the righteousness of good works contrasted with the righteousness of Christ received by faith.

The second half of the passage speaks of the Christian life

1. The goal
2. The effort
3. The encouragements

For a Family Service talk you could develop the picture of the race, with drawings of
The runner - the Christian living for God
The finishing line - the end of a life lived with God
The prize - life with God for ever

Why not interview one of the sportsmen in the congregation (wearing their kit?) about the effort involved in training, the commitment needed, the feeling of achievement etc. as a way of illustrating the passage.

The prayer-time should include praise for all the "gains" of the Christian life but also prayer for those who miss out on that because of their desire to save themselves or their following of the way of the world. Church Family Worship Sections 24 and 30 may be of help and suitable hymns and songs will be found in the list overleaf.

5 Group Sheet

Gains & losses

Philippians 3.1-21

AIM To renew the vision of that whole-hearted commitment to Christ which is essential if we are to experience to the full the joy of Christian living.

BEGIN HERE
Imagine your home has been destroyed by a fire.
Which three things would you most regret losing, and why?
Discuss your answers in small groups.

BIBLE STUDY
READ PHILIPPIANS 3.1-21

Losses
What does the passage tell us about Paul's life before he became a Christian? (vv.1-6) Why did he count it all as loss? (vv.7-8) What sort of things must we count as loss in order to experience Christ's life? Are they all bad things?

How do twentieth century English people put "confidence in the flesh"?

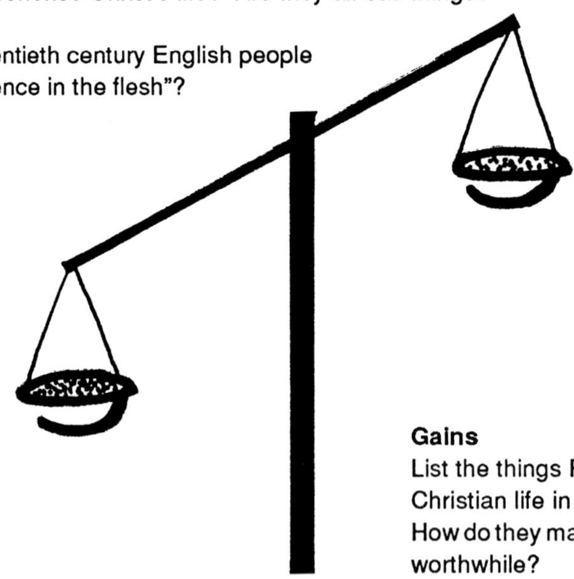

Gains
List the things Paul speaks of as 'gains' in the Christian life in verses 8-11.
How do they make the Christian life positive and worthwhile?

What was Paul's great aim in life - can you sum this up in less than fifty words?

How do all the 'gains' spur us on in our Christian living?

ACTION
Ask group members to write a list of their aims or targets in life as a Christian. After a few minutes ask them to put a tick by those they are making progress with, a question mark by those they are a little stuck over and a cross by those where things are not going too well. Share your answers and discuss ways in which you can help each other.

ADDITIONAL QUESTIONS

Losses

- How can our religion or our family background get in the way of our relationship with God?
- Why do people often prefer the way of earning salvation through good works to the way of receiving it by faith?
- What things in our lives are barriers to our knowledge of Christ and should, therefore, be counted as loss?
- How does Paul describe the non-Christian way of life in vv.18-19?
  What are its consequences? What examples of that way of life can you think of in today's world?

Gains

- What does Paul mean by "the righteousness from God that depends on faith"? (v.9)
- How does Christ's resurrection power change our lives?
- In what ways does the picture of the athlete help us understand the Christian life? (vv.12-14).
- How does Paul describe the future of God's people?

WORSHIP AND PRAYER

During a time of praise you could ask the group to contribute short prayers beginning with the words "Jesus has given me .....". If your group enjoys singing you could ask them to supply verses for Mission Praise 527 (Oh! Oh! Oh! How good is the Lord), saying "He gives me ....".

Pray about the targets in our Christian living shared earlier during the discussion.

Songs in Mission Praise which could be used include:

7 Alleluia
17 Be thou my vision
59 Glorious things of thee are spoken
63 Guide me, O thou great Jehovah
84 I have decided to follow Jesus
118 Jesus how lovely you are
127 Jesus take me as I am
162 My hope is built on nothing less
204 Sing alleluia to the Lord
214 Take time to be holy
235 There's a sound on the wind
285 Above the voices of the world around me
408 I delight greatly in the Lord
410 I get so excited, Lord
415 I live, I live because he is risen
459 Jesus you are changing me
473 Lift up your heads
527 Oh! Oh! Oh! How good is the Lord
542 Reconciled, I'm reconciled.

More Learning Activities

5

Philippians 3.1-21

INTRODUCTION

The passage deals with those things which Paul gave up as rubbish when compared with the value of knowing Christ. If we read between the lines we may also catch a glimpse of some of the enemies of the gospel.

- ACTIVITY 1
  MAGIC SHOP

This exercise does not attempt to mirror Paul's experience but will get the group into thinking about what they personally value and how much they value it. It might be a useful lead-in to the passage and should be played before looking at the text of Philippians.

The group gets into pairs, one choosing to be **A** and the other **B**. **A** is a shopkeeper of a very special shop. This shop sells everything and anything. If you want it, the shopkeeper has it, even if it is somewhere in a box in the back room. His wares include not just objects but intangibles as well - a knighthood; a perfect figure; to win the Olympic 400 metres; a voice like Placido Domingo; lots of friends. **B** enters the shop and asks for something. At this point the game can be played fairly lightly but it will make for quite a different experience if **B** asks for something he or she REALLY would like.

A stocks this item, of course. **A** stocks everything. But it comes at a price. However the price is never money. So **B** might want to win an Olympic medal but **A** may set the price at "having to live in the Outer Hebrides for ten years". Perhaps **B** is happy with this and agrees. But if **A** raises the price as "having to live in the Outer Hebrides for ten years OR having raging toothache for five years" **B** may think the medal isn't worth it and backs off. **A** must then adjust the price downwards or he will lose the sale. They continue to haggle until they reach an agreement. "This item for this price".

A and **B** then reverse roles and repeat the exercise. When all the pairs have finished each person announces what he or she has bought and what they were prepared to pay for it. It is possible that some people may not want to say anything. Their reticence must be respected, of course.

The leader should pick up this kind of question:
"In what way was this game like and unlike life?"
"How realistic was your final bargain?"
"Would you really be prepared to pay that price for that item?"
"What different sorts of cost were charged?"
"Are some costs harder to take than others?'"
"What kind of demand finally made you back out of the agreement?"

(This exercise is adapted from P.Gordon and H.A.Davison, Games and Simulations in Education.)

5

- **ACTIVITY 2
PLUS POINTS**

Paul lists a hand of seven trump cards. "Circumcised the eight day, of the people of Israel, of the tribe of Benjamin..." etc. Once in his life he would have played these cards and flattened the opposition. He "scores points" by reason of his race and tribe, his religious upbringing, his moral righteousness and his spiritual zeal. Every way you look at Paul he is about perfect.

The group divides into twos and threes. The task is to produce a hand of seven cards which will beat Paul's. Invent a character (male or female) and give them qualities which together will make a rock-crusher of a hand when they come to play spiritual poker again Paul. Try to reflect the same range of "virtues" - impeccable pedigree, unimpeachable references, unsurpassable zeal, unequalled achievements. ("Baptised by the Archbishop of Canterbury in water flown specially (by Concorde) from the River Jordan").

This game is a caricature of the way we sometimes think. That is exactly its point. When the various 'hands' have been disclosed, the leader might like to play 'recording angel' and award a prize to the best one. But then the group should be taken back to Philippians 3.7-11 and reflect on the fact that ALL these qualities are to be considered rubbish compared with the value of knowing Christ. At the end of the discussion, it might make Paul's point more clearly if the pieces of paper are collected in, screwed up and literally put in the waste-paper basket.

- **ACTIVITY 3
HE'S THE REAL THING**

What did it mean to Paul to "know Christ"? Why was knowing Him a "surpassing greatness"? In verses 10 and 11 he starts to unpack the bundle labelled "knowing Christ". It means experiencing his resurrection power here on earth, sharing in suffering like his, knowing that he would rise to new life beyond the grave etc.

Working in small groups, members take a large piece of paper and unpack the bundle "knowing Christ". To do this, they brainstorm on the idea and put any words or phrases inside the bundle which they feel are involved in "knowing Christ". It is these bundles which are worth more than the 'rubbish' of our achievements. The final products might well become material for a time of praise and worship.

- **ACTIVITY 4**
  ARE YOU A FLESH TRUSTER? (A SELF ANALYSIS)

Divide the group into sub-groups of three or four, and give them a copy of this questionnaire. They have 25 mins to fill it in. Suggest that everyone has five minutes to read it through and make their own personal choice, and then for the next 20 minutes discuss in the groups a common choice they all agree on. Then as a group share the results and the reasons for the choices people have made.

1. You apply for a job with a Christian organisation, and you want to indicate in your letter of application that your Christian credentials are second to none - ***Do you ...***

☐ Tell them the name of your (well known) church, date of Baptism (by a well known minister), the fact that you are a house group host and you sing in the choir.

☐ Give a brief testimony of your conversion and subsequent Christian experience, avoiding mentioning the fact that you were converted through a rather extreme house church grouping which you left several years ago.

☐ Say that you have been a Christian for the past 6 years and while you are not perfect you do try to live a truly Christian life. You go to church regularly.

2. Your friend calls to you over the garden fence one day and says that she has read in the church magazine (which goes round all the villages) that the church (to which you go) needs people for the flower rota. She tells you she is thinking of volunteering although she doesn't go to church. 'I don't think God worries whether you go to church or not'. ***Do you reply...***

☐ " Well...if you ask me, anyone who does anything in the church must first become a member or at least attend worship regularly. Doing things for God doesn't make you a Christian it is what you believe that counts. God is not interested in what you do for him but what he can do for you. So you ought to come to church first."

☐ "Wonderful idea, come and do the flowers I am sure Mrs Shah will be pleased to have some help. I used to do that when I first started in the church, but I now do the prayers and readings so I came off the flower rota. I really feel I am close to God when I am standing up the front. Perhaps you will eventually want to come to a church service too."

☐ "Oh, I wouldn't get involved in that. What you need to do is to come to the Bible Study we have every week at the Vicarage. We have such a wonderful time. Do you know I go to three Bible studies a week now, the one on Thursday afternoons, the one on Monday lunchtime, and I go to house group too."

3. It is time for the annual church party. You are a member of the PCC, and when it is discussed, it is proposed that this year instead of the usual practice of providing sandwiches and cake, there is a slap-up meal, with wine, starter, the works, organised by an ex-chef. You know it will be good but also expensive. ***Do you:***

☐ Side with the person who says it should be turned into a hunger meal and the money sent to Tear Fund, on the grounds that the church has no right to be extravagant.

☐ Think about suggesting a compromise which won't price some people out of the evening, but reflect on the likelihood of a feast and reflect that Christians ought to be able to enjoy themselves and anyway it might bring a few of the fringe people in - like your squash partner. So you vote in favour.

☐ Volunteer to be in charge of the wine buying. You have a little known weakness for fine Bulgarian wines. In any case it is right for Christians to celebrate, they did it with vigour in the Old Testament. Anyway we should encourage the ex-chef he is a new Christian and it is something he can do for God, you feel.

● ACTIVITY 5
ROGUES GALLERY

Reading between the lines is a fascinating exercise. As we look at Phil.3 we get a sense of the sort of Christians who were a trial to Paul and who in different ways had misunderstood or were distorting the gospel.

The group's job is to produce vivid, visual portraits of these types in the style of the Mister Men or Happy Families. Paul gives us the first century version. The group must produce twentieth century equivalents.

1. **Jeremy and Jennifer,**
   or Mr Judaizer
   (vv1-11)(Eric or Ethel Effort)

They "put confidence in the flesh"; trusting in things like circumcision, personal morality, keeping the law of Moses, their birth and background rather than in God's free forgiveness through Christ.

2. **Peter and Pauline, or Miss Perfect**
   (vv12-17)(Arry or Anthea Arrived)

Sure that they have "arrived" or "obtained" and are already perfect, they feel no great need to press on in the Christian life because God has done it all. They are happy with living on past experience of God or at least where they are at the moment.

3. **Nigel and Nora**
   or Mrs Anti-Nomian
   (vv17-21)(Fred or Flora Free)

They live their lives not bothered about living in a Christ-like way. They are forgiven, after all, so what does it matter? Their "god is their belly"; "they glory in their shame"; so they "set their minds on earthly things".

Encourage the groups to express the personalities of these characters by exaggerating their features and limbs, giving them appropriate objects to hold and appropriate clothes to wear (eg rose coloured spectacles; a wooden spoon etc). Make sure they label all the bits with explanatory notes. And tell them not to be afraid of making their efforts funny or bizarre. We're aiming for bold cartoons.

6

Facing the pressures

Philippians 4

AIM To see that "In the Lord" we are given strength to stand firm against the various pressures we face.

INTRODUCTION

The conclusions of Paul's epistles are rather like a letter which finishes with a P.S. followed by P.P.S. and then P.P.P.S. as he jots down all the extra thoughts and personal encouragements which he wants to pass on to his readers. It isn't always easy to study such a mixed jumble of thoughts. The one theme which does give some unity to the passage is that of the pressures we face - problems in relationships, worry over personal circumstances, the pressure of temptation, the needs we have which must be met. Paul was no stranger to such pressures himself but found strength to cope "in the Lord" (a phrase which comes up frequently in this passage). He urges his readers to "stand firm in the Lord", "agree in the Lord", "rejoice in the Lord" and so on.

This week's study begins with an exercise which helps the group think how they react to pressure; then it looks at Paul's encouragement to us as we face such pressures and concludes with a time in which group members can encourage one another concerning the current difficulties which they are facing.

NOTES

v.1 Paul's pastoral concern is shown once again here. His encouragement echoes that in 1.27.

vv.2-3 Euodia and Syntyche appear to have been part of the group who worked with Paul. We don't know who the "true yokefellow" was unless 'Syzygus' (the Greek word for yokefellow) is his proper name and Paul is calling on him to be true to that name in bringing these two together.

"The book of life" is the record of those who belong to God (see Revelation 20.12-15). It is like the register of citizens kept by a city such as Philippi.

v.5 Forbearance is the considerate thoughtfulness for others which gives way out of courtesy.

"The Lord is near" - Paul is probably thinking of the expectation of his return, rather than his constant presence.

v.6 "Anxiety is an attempt to carry the burden of the future oneself, prayer is leaving it in the safe hands of God. Thanksgiving for past benefits is the surest road to confidence in future ones." (G.B. Caird).

v.7 Inward peace flows from our relationship with God. It keeps guard over our hearts and minds protecting them from fear and worry. The Greek word for 'keep' suggests a garrison guarding a city.

vv.8-9 These qualities are not especially Christian ones but are the virtues of those who are morally upright. The Christian should pay attention to what is good - whether it is seen in non-Christian or Christian (like Paul who had handed on the Christian faith to them and who sought to embody it in his life).

v.10 Paul begins here to speak tactfully of his gratitude for their support. He doesn't want to give them any feeling that he expected their support or that he was not grateful for the help they had given.

There had been some delay in them sending their gifts - probably because they were unable to do so because they were fairly poor themselves.

vv.11-12 Paul worked on the principle of supporting himself and so making the Gospel available without charge (so he could not be criticised as many American tele-evangelists have been) even if this meant going without sometimes. (See 2 Corinthians 11.23-29 for a picture of the hardships he willingly suffered for the sake of the Gospel).

v.13 Paul's strength comes not from himself but from the Lord who gives him strength in his weakness (See 2 Corinthians 12.9-10).

v.14 Paul is not ungrateful for their gift. He especially values the concern it shows .

vv.15-17 Paul speaks of their financial support in terms of a commercial investment in the cause of promoting the Gospel. He received material support - they received spiritual blessing. It will produce rich dividends in the service of the Kingdom. God will reward them for their generosity.

v.15 Paul cannot be thinking of his Gospel-preaching only beginning after he left Philippi, so he must be thinking of it from the point of view of his relationship with the Philippians. He is referring to the early days of his missionary work after leaving Macedonia.

v.18 The metaphor changes from that of commerce to that of sacrifice which pleases God.

v.19 The Philippians may well have impoverished themselves in giving to Paul - but Paul assures them of the generosity of God's provision, on a scale befitting his wealth. As always in Paul's thinking, God's generosity takes place within the context of our relationship with Christ.

v.20 The God who meets our needs is our Father, who provides for the needs of all his children. The joy of this doxology has been seen throughout this epistle.

v.21 This is the one place where Paul uses the word "saint" in the singular to speak of God's people (see 1.1).

v.22 Caesar's household means the slaves and freedmen who worked for the Emperor, some of whom may well have had contact with members of the church in Philippi.

SUNDAY EXTRA

There is a diversity of themes in this closing section of Philippians - with enough material for a series of sermons! Some of them may have been touched on as earlier passages were looked at - such as the problem of disagreement or our support for Christian workers. This week's service might concentrate on vv. 4-8 and the call to rejoice in the Lord, give thanks and pray. Some of the outcomes of such a pattern are seen in later verses. We can experience God's peace (v. 7), power (v. 13) and provision (v. 19).

For a Family Service talk on a similar theme begin with a worried face like the one on this week's Group Page. Ask people why this person might be worried - add arrows with their suggestions. Go on to ask what we can do when we are worried. Talk about verses 4-6 and the way we can pray and praise (you could use a drawing of an appropriate face). Lead in to God's promise of peace (use a drawing of a peaceful, happy face). Relate this promise to some of the situations suggested earlier and recap on the way God can change things.

Clearly structure the prayer time to include the various aspects of praise (rejoicing), thanksgiving, prayer for others and prayer for ourselves. Paul's encouragements to rejoice in the Lord make an extended time of praise appropriate this week.

Church Family Worship section 13 is about the Life of Prayer. Other hymns and songs are listed in the Worship and Prayer section.

Group Sheet 6

Facing the pressures

Philippians 4

AIM To see that "In Christ" we are given strength to stand firm against the various pressures we face.

BEGIN HERE

People, like things, react to pressure in different ways.
Which best describes you? Share your answers in pairs.
Do you -

Explode - like a bomb
or Implode - and turn in on yourself
or Collapse in a heap
or Suddenly topple over when the pressure gets too tough
or Get tossed about hither and thither
or Sway in the wind but stay in one piece
or Stand firm despite it all

BIBLE STUDY

READ PHILIPPIANS 4

DISAGREEMENT

Imagine Euodia and Syntyche belong to your church - what might have caused their disagreements? How would you go about helping them to agree? (vv 2-3)

WORRY

What things cause us to worry? How can God help us cope with those worries? (vv 4-7)

TEMPTATION

How do outside influences from things we read, watch, see in the world create pressure on us? How can Paul's advice in verses 8-9 help us as we face the pressures of the media and the world around us?

NEED

In what ways do changes in our circumstances affect us? What can we learn from the way Paul coped with both need and plenty? When have we received help from others? (vv10-20)

ACTION

Ask everyone to share in small groups the area (or areas) of pressure which shake them most. Then spend time encouraging one another to "stand firm in the Lord" (v.1)- perhaps by sharing how God has helped in similar situations and by praying for one another.

ADDITIONAL QUESTIONS

Disagreement

- Paul doesn't spell out exactly what the problem was between Euodia and Syntyche - doctrinal? ethical? ecclesiastical? personal? - the trouble was not that they had disagreed but that they had caused a division in the church. What is the difference between disagreement and division? Is disagreement wrong? What should we do when there is disagreement?

- Are there divisions in your church? What causes division? What can we do to see that divisions do not occur? How do we heal divisions?

Worry

- How can we possibly rejoice when everything is going wrong?
- How does God's peace keep guard in our hearts and minds?

Temptation

- What examples can you think of the good things Paul encourages us to concentrate on?

Need

- How much is our contentment dependent on outward circumstances? What makes us discontent? What is the "secret" of being content? Would you be content in Paul's circumstances?

- Why was Paul reluctant to rely on the help of others? (See 1 Corinthians 9.1-18) What does Paul value most about the support of the Philippians? What does this passage teach about the value of Christian giving?

PRAYER AND WORSHIP

The small group sharing should finish with prayer for each other in those groups. After that bring the whole group together and ask them to think of one main lesson they have learnt from Philippians. After a pause for thought ask them to join in short prayers of thanksgiving for those things. Having prayed earlier about the pressures faced by the group you may want to pray for others under stress. Pray too for any Christian workers whom you support.

Songs and hymns could include any of the following (taken as usual from Mission Praise).

29	Christ is the answer	312	Be bold, be strong
49	Do not be afraid	339	Draw near to God
45	Father, I place into your hands	347	Father, although I cannot see
76	How firm a foundation	400	How precious, O Lord
92	I need thee every hour	409	I do not know what lies ahead
183	Peace is flowing like a river	457	Jesus put this song into our hearts
194	Rejoice in the Lord always	497	My peace I give unto you
233	There's a quiet understanding	527	Oh! Oh! Oh! How good is the Lord
262	What a friend we have in Jesus	538	Peace I give to you
269	When we walk with the Lord	543	Rejoice! Rejoice! Christ is in you

More Learning Activities

6

Philippians 4

INTRODUCTION

This chapter deals with a number of isolated issues.

- **Conflict between two members.**
- **A hint of pressure on the church from the outside.**
- **An exhortation to concentrate on what is good.**
- **And insight into the support of missionaries.**

- ACTIVITY 1
THE PCC AT PHILIPPI

The group becomes the Parochial Church Council (or Elders' meeting) at Philippi considering a number of vital issues in the light of Paul's letter which has just arrived carried by Epaphroditus. You will need a chairperson and at least enough members for the role cards A-E to be distributed one per person. These five roles are "planted" to ensure that the discussion gets going and that different views are represented. The rest of the group members will play themselves. It is important, however, that the "plants" stick to the role they have been given. There will be time at the end to come clean about their real views.
(The role cards can be photocopied).

Afterwards you need to talk over the PCC meeting, particularly if the "plants" have thrown themselves into the debate! The leader will want to give members a chance to say how realistic they found the exercise. What emotions were aroused? How DO Christians resolve conflicts like these? How SHOULD they?

Some Groups may feel that the activity does not call for any reference to the Bible. Its aim is to force group members to apply Paul's teaching to specific situations. In fact, most of what Paul says in Chapter 4 is found somewhere in somebody's brief.

The agenda is as follows:

1. Women's Fellowship report
2. The Riverside Cafe
3. The Youth Fellowship Drama Group
4. Missions Committee Report

CHAIRPERSON'S NOTES

1. **Women's Fellowship**

The basic problem is that two of the most active women in the group, Euodia and Syntyche, are at loggerheads. Apparently, Euodia spoke slightingly about the flower display for which Syntyche had been responsible. Now the Women's Fellowship is divided into two camps. Euodia is an assertive woman, with a heart of gold but inclined to call a spade a spade. Syntyche is a tireless worker, not terribly vocal, but determined to get her own way in any enterprise in which she is involved. As chairman you'd like the PCC to come to a decision about a constructive way forward but you know that like the Women's Fellowship the PCC has also begun to take sides.

2. **The Riverside Drop -In Centre**

Lydia, the wealthy businesswoman, set up The Riverside (soon after Paul's first visit) as a "drop in" centre and means of evangelistic outreach. It has been remarkably successful. The civic authorities have just announced a new development which will involve building on the present riverside site. The compensation suggested is derisory. The PCC have been asked to make a decision about how it will respond.

3. **The Youth Fellowship Drama Group**

The young people at Philippi are zealous in their concern to evangelise the city. As part of their programme they are putting on an excerpt from "The Outcast" a play by Menander. It reveals in graphic detail the emptiness of a life without Christ. You have heard however that it contains a number of swear words and a scene involving a scantily clad dancing girl. Some church members are anxious about the propriety of such a production and ask for a PCC ruling.

4. **Missions Committee Report**

You have been supporting Paul for some while now, through gifts taken in person by Epaphroditus. You now need to decide whether you will continue at the same level of giving (roughly 8% of your total income) or cut back or increase.

Role Card A

Item1: You are a spiritual person. You think it's time Euodia was told (lovingly, of course) that she should temper her honest and frank remarks. An official reprimand from the PCC would do her no end of good.

Item 2: It is vital to have a half night of prayer about this crisis. You have no other ideas on the matter. But you will keep on pushing for a half night of prayer until the PCC agrees.

Item 3: You are very worried about the sound of this. Paul says you should think on things which are "true, honourable, just, pure, lovely...." Stop the play.

Item 4: You are in favour of the biggest increase the PCC can make. You strongly believe as Paul says, " my God will supply every need of yours according to his riches in Christ."

Role Card B:

Item 1: You think of yourself as a bit of a realist. You dislike Syntyche intensely. In fact you have a letter which Euodia showed you in tears which indicates that the week previous to this quarrel Syntyche has complained about the behaviour of Euodia's son in Sunday School hinting that he was an indulged little brat who needed discipline. You think Syntyche should be reprimanded.

Item 2: In your view the authorities will continue to take and take until the church stands up to them.

Item 3: You know Paul said that you should think on those things which were "true, honorable, just, pure lovely..." but everything has to be seen in context. The intention of this play is to show the emptiness of life without Christ. Even the Bible contains reports of David's adultery and Salome's dance. You think the young people should be allowed to continue.

Item 4: Paul's in prison and likely to be executed. Hardly worth budgetting for. You want to make this point but in as tactful and "Christian" way possible.

Role Card C:

Item 1: You are a bit retiring but pleasant and tactful. You have worked with both women on a number of missions and think highly of them. They have different personalities but you believe that with tactful handling they can be reconciled. You are sure that confrontation will do no good.

Item 2: You are quite sure that in trials of every kind the proper thing to do is to praise God and pray. "The peace of God will keep your hearts." "Have no anxiety about anything."

Item 3: Your son is in the young people's drama group.

Item 4: You are privately worried about what will be said in Thessalonica and Beroea if they get to hear that your PCC has cut back on its support for Paul.

Role Card D:

Item 1: You pride yourself on being outspoken. You know all about this and privately think that it could have been settled long ago if Clement (a PCC member) had done his duty and confronted them both. You think he has been rather cowardly and intend pointing this out to him. The work of God is suffering because Clement has been so spineless.

Item 2: You are furious about the high handed behaviour of the civic fathers. There is no point in sitting down under it. It's time to protest! "Forbearance" does not mean being a doormat!

Item 3: Take any view you wish as long as you are abrasive about it.

Item 4: You are angry that this item should even be debated. How people can consider not increasing support for Paul after all he has done for the christians at Philippi etc etc.

Role Card E:

Item 1: This is really an internal matter for the Women's Fellowship. You feel it should not have been referred to the PCC at all.

Item 2: If Paul says "let your forbearance be known to all men" then you are against any kind of protest. In any case you believe that Christ may come again soon and there is little point getting worked up about any project in the light of his return. 'The Lord is at hand'.

Item 3: You studied Menander for A level. He is a world famous dramatist.

Item 4: You are not sure there is much point in increasing support for Paul. There are many needs in Philippi and in any case Paul has said, "I have learned in whatever state I am, to be content."It sounds as if he doesn't need the money anyway.

6

ACTIVITY 2
THE LOST ENDING

Amazingly, a fragment of the lost ending of the letter to the Philippians has recently been discovered. It is about four verses long but deals with a topic of great concern to Christians who live in the 1990's.

The group divides into smaller groups of threes or fours. They are given one of the following topics and asked to reconstruct the last four verses of Philippians. Each group works on a different topic, but the idea is to write in the style of St. Paul the sort of thing he would have said on ...

Pop music
TV soap operas
Credit cards
Old people
Family Services
Income Tax

ACTIVITY 3
LOVE FROM ...

The task is to design a card with a wish and a verse from anywhere in Philippians. A piece of paper folded in half will do as the card. It will need a design, or rough drawing, on the cover, a wish on the inside right page, and a verse from Philippians on the inside left-hand page. No verse may be used more than once. Try to make the design, wish and verse appropriate to the recipient. The cards are to be sent to ... The President of the USSR; the Prime Minister; your vicar; any member of your family; yourself at the end of a bad week; someone in your home group; Terry Waite (or someone in the same situation). Ask the members of the group to produce cards for some, or all, of these.

Other help for group leaders from CPAS

- **Open House Magazine**
  The only magazine produced exclusively for leaders of small groups, including home and house groups. For further details contact the Adult Training and Resources Unit.

- In the same series have you tried **Project Matthew** and **Project Acts?** Available from CPAS, Sales Unit.

- For material suitable for Women's groups write to **Ministry Among Women Unit.**

- For Young People and Children's groups contact our **Youth and Children Division.**

For further information about any of the above please write to:

CPAS
Athena Drive
Tachbrook Park
WARWICK
CV34 6NG
Tel: (0926) 334242